Freedom in a Framework:

Some Possibilities with Series 3

by

Richard More
Assistant Curate of Macclesfield Parish Church, Cheshire

GROVE BOOKS

BRAMCOTE   NOTTS.

CONTENTS

	Page
Introduction	3
1. The Two Extremes	4
2. Words into Action	7
3. The Word and The Prayers	12
4. The Communion	16
5. What about Children?	21
6. Series 3 plus	23

Copyright Richard More 1975

ACKNOWLEDGMENT

Quotations from Series 3 Holy Communion, from *A Commentary on Holy Communion Series 3,* and from *The Presentation of the Eucharist* are all made by permission of the S.P.C.K. London (and, in the case of Series 3, of the Registrars of the Provinces of Canterbury and York).

First Impression November 1975

ISSN 0305 3067

ISBN 0 901710 78 4

INTRODUCTION

It is now almost three years since Series 3 Holy Communion came into general use in the Church of England. This booklet seeks to share some of the possibilities and methods of presentation that people have found valuable in their use of the service over this time. I would like to thank those who responded to my request for ideas in the Church press. They will see many of their suggestions in what follows. I have written in the main considering the use of the service in a parish situation for a weekly Sunday Parish Communion. I realize that for some people my suggestions will seem very staid, while for others they will seem hopelessly 'trendy.' That's life! In all I am not trying to demonstrate 'what you can get away with under the guise of Series 3' but have sought to suggest some basic principles that I believe need to be considered by the congregation that decides to use this new type of flexible liturgical text.

I know that the editor of *News of Liturgy* would always be pleased to hear of further such examples of the use of Series 3.

Richard More

October 1975

1. THE TWO EXTREMES

'It hath been the wisdom of the Church of England ever since the first compiling of her publick Liturgy, to keep the mean between the two extremes, of too much stiffness in refusing, and in too much easiness in admitting any variation from it.'

So begins the Preface to the revision of *The Book of Common Prayer* in 1662, in which the writer is seeking to account for the alterations that have been made to the Prayer Book, when it returned to public use after the Commonwealth. This sentence takes on an entirely new meaning if it is applied to the current liturgical situation in the Church of England. In 1662 the 'Anglican compromise' was taking place in London amongst the bishops and the landowners in parliament. For us the compromise has moved to the parish church to be worked out by the Vicar and the P.C.C. The Alternative Services Measure, and the services authorized under it, introduced a radically different approach to the use of liturgical texts in the Church of England.

The Prayer Books of Edward VI may have been very different in content from the Sarum Missal which they replaced, yet they maintained the same basic approach concerning their function. They came as 'meals on wheels'. The recipients of meals on wheels have merely to wait for the meal to arrive. The menu is chosen for them, and the food is purchased, prepared and cooked centrally. It is then delivered to local areas and served on the plate; the recipients are required merely to eat it! And there is no local cook, merely a well-drilled waiter. Thus the Sarum Missal instructed the priest as to what he was to do as he celebrated the Mass: what he was to read and when, where he was to stand, when he was to genuflect or make the sign of the cross. The complexities and variations that existed (which Cranmer sought to rationalize) were not those introduced by the priest on local initiative, but the jungle of seasonal ceremonies and variations included in the written liturgy.

Cranmer and those who revised his work in the seventeenth century adopted the same principle, namely that the Prayer Book instructs the priest in how to conduct the service of Holy Communion. He has merely to do what he is told. He is instructed what to say and when, where to stand, what to wear—somewhat in the manner of a detailed film-script. Nothing is required of the priest and congregation other than obedience (and the Holy Spirit!!). The only variations that existed between services were the collects and readings, the homily or sermon, and on five festivals the proper prefaces.[1] The only decision that rested with the priest was the content of the sermon, whether to read the exhortation when he saw the people 'negligent to come to the Holy Communion', and which of the two collects for the King and of the two post-communion prayers to use.

So it was, with this moderate amount of seasonal variation and this mini-mum of local choice, that the liturgical meal was dispatched in England

---

[1] This amount of seasonal variation was considerably greater than that permitted by some continental reformers. Zwingli had only one set of readings in his service at Zurich.

until the passing of the Alternative Services Measure in 1965. However, meals on wheels, though very easy for the consumer, are often criticized. Some people find parts to be stodgy, others wish to add spice, others even to alter the taste. And so it was with the Prayer Book. Parts were often omitted—the longer exhortation to worthy reception, the Ten Commandments, the Collect for the King; they were stodgy. Spice was added in the form of hymns, psalms and anthems, the summary of the law, responses to the gospel, the Benedictus and Agnus Dei. Ceremonial was added to alter the appearance (and the taste??). And nearly all separated the main course (Holy Communion) from the other courses of Morning Prayer and the Litany.

The abortive revision of 1927/28 was an attempt to add some of these popular ingredients to the basic dish to render it more appetising. But this was not the answer to the problem and so it failed.

With the Alternative Services Measure a new approach was adopted, and the written liturgy assumed a new role. No longer is it solely provided centrally for the priest and people to perform as a drill. Now the basic materials are supplied to be moulded and used. As one might purchase a packet of frozen food, which needs to be thawed and cooked before it can be consumed, so with the written liturgy! Certainly, it comes with instructions on the packet. At first we read them carefully because we are unsure. Gradually we become familiar with the contents, their mood and flavour. The instructions become unnecessary as we gain confidence. The meal reflects our own creation and has the distinctive marks of our tastes and skill; while keeping the goodness and basic flavour of the material with which we began.

This principle of moulding the rite to a particular situation is in fact what has always been done in practice from the days of Elizabeth I. It is true, as a recent writer in the *Church Times* claimed, that a plea for 1662 is always in practice a plea for 1662 'as it is used in this parish'. Such use is only technically legal because of the provisions of the 1965 Measure, now replaced by the Worship and Doctrine Measure—the Measure which the same people often dislike because it is seen as destroying that uniformity of worship and doctrine within the Church of England that Cranmer had sought to establish.

However, it would be both highly cynical and also untrue to imagine that the vast number of options and the flexibility permitted in the written text is merely the Church saying that uniformity is now impossible and so the aim is to make anything legal. Certainly one of the original purposes of the 1927-8 proposals had been to bring a large amount of current practice under the law (but clearly to exclude other practice). In the same way the immediate authorization of much 1928 material in the form of Series I can be seen as having this motive.[1]

---

1 This was evidenced by Lord Ramsey who in presenting the service said 'It is not a work of revision so much as a work of current authorization.'

But this is not the purpose behind the form adopted in Series 2/3. Both Series 2 and 3 have introduced a new form of written liturgy. A major change can be seen in the format and purpose of rubrics. Previously, they were detailed instructions and legally binding on the priest; failure to observe them could result in prosecution. Much could be and has been written on their interpretation. In many situations the rubric was as important in the text as the words to be spoken. Thus most of the alterations made to the Communion service in 1662 were alterations in rubrics which have often been seen as altering the theology of the service, as for example in the introduction of the manual acts and the instructions about the disposal of what remains of the consecrated Bread and Wine. Rubrics in the new services are much shorter and come more in the style of stage directions in a play. The classic example of the new style of rubric is 'Note' number 13 at the beginning.

> *'Hymns, Notices, Offerings of the People*
>
> 'Points are indicated for the singing of hymns, the publication of banns of marriage and other notices, and the collection and presentation of the offerings of the people; but if occasion requires there are other points at which they may occur.'

All of which means there are specified places in which these items are particularly appropriate, but in the end you may have them where you like!

The one rubric that perhaps can be seen as having theological significance and as such is mandatory is that at 25 'The President takes the bread and wine'.[1]

The new services place a great responsibility onto the priest and congregation. Much detailed preparation now becomes essential before the written text can be used for an act of worship. A basic liturgical knowledge is also a necessity, so that the purpose of the text is clearly understood by those using it. Every priest is now a liturgist.

The mandatory material should ensure the necessary doctrinal control over the contents of the service, while it is the responsibility of the local church to ensure that the worship reflects not only the worship and teaching of the Church of England but also the particular gifts, interests and character of the particular congregation assembled that day.

[1] See page 17.

2. WORDS INTO ACTION

We come now to look at how Series 3 might be put into practice as an act or worship, and to examine some of the issues that need to be considered, not merely when the service is first introduced, but in the on-going week by week celebration.

Some people enjoy sarcastically demonstrating the infinite variations that the written text permits. It would be possible to have a service radically different in content each week, but clearly nobody would want this. There are, however, two dangers that can be encountered in the general use of the optional material.

1. *The danger of constant change* whereby people are never certain what is going to happen next. The basic structure of the service must be constant, to the extent that people will know whether there are to be 2 or 3 readings and when the hymns will occur. Many people need to feel at ease in worship so that fellowship with God and each other is facilitated by the words used and this will not be possible if they are on edge. This is a different thing from the freedom enjoyed in 'charismatic' worship, where singing, prophecy etc. is normally within the clear structure of the service. A sense of unease will inevitably be present when the service is first introduced, but should quickly be overcome.

2. *The danger of no variety* which can happen when one selection of options is chosen when the service is first introduced and these are never altered. This results in certain possibilities never being tried. The Liturgical Commission commented on this in connection with the way that Series 2 had been used in some parishes.

> 'They have never really *experimented* with the various options and all too often their experiences has been limited to only one form of service. Furthermore, whereas they have been able to adapt themselves perhaps with difficulty—to a particular set of changes involved in Series 2, they have not always been aware of the larger adjustment required to *living with change.*'[1]

This can be a danger if one prints (with permission!) one's own version of the service omitting the material which is not going to be used. It does enable people to follow the service with much greater ease, but can rule out a number of options that might have been required later.

[1] *A Commentary on Holy Communion Series 3* (S.P.C.K., 1971) p.5—[hereafter called 'Commentary'].

The Mandatory Material

This is indicated by black numbers in the margin, and is less than many people might assume.

6	Collect of the Day
7 or 9	Old Testament lesson or epistle
11	Gospel
13	Creed (Sundays or Holy days)
15	Prayers
17-19	Penitence
24	Placing of the bread and wine
25	The Taking of the bread and wine
26-29	The Thanksgiving
30	The Breaking of the Bread
31	The Lord's Prayer
32-33	The Giving of the Bread and the Cup
39 or 40	Prayer of Thanks
43	Dismissal

It is interesting to compare this list of the 'minimum required' with that produced by the interdenominational Joint Liturgical Group in their booklet *Initiation and Eucharist* which was published in 1972 just before Series 3 came into use, and in which three members of the Liturgical Commission (including the Chairman, Dean Jasper) took part. They outline the normative structure of the total liturgy as follows:

Old Testament Reading[1]
New Testament Reading(s)
Sermon[2]
Intercession
The Thanksgiving
The Communion

In *Initiation and Eucharist* this normative structure is followed by a possible basic pattern which very clearly relates to Series 3 but not in every respect. Two notable omissions are The Peace and the Creed. Concerning the Peace they merely state that if it is to be used, then it should be included in the context of the supper. The Creed comes off less well.

> 'The recital of the might acts of God in the eucharistic prayer fulfills the necessary purpose of credal proclamation. The use of the Creed is thus in no way essential, though it may have value as an act of corporate participation in a summation of the Faith partly declared in the Scripture Readings. If it is to be used, this should occur before the action of the Supper is begun'.[3]

[1] It is interesting that Series 3 does not regard an Old Testament reading as mandatory except on 9 Sundays each year—the last 5 in Trinity and the 4 Sundays in Advent.
[2] The 'note' about the sermon in Series 3 states that a sermon should be preached whenever possible but is not necessary at every service.
[3] *Initiation and Eucharist* editors N. Clarke and R. C. D. Jasper (S.P.C.K., 1972) pp. 29-30.

It needs to be remembered that the Creed has historically played a distinctive part in Church of England worship.

This 'Possible Basic Pattern' also varies from Series 3 in the position of the Penitence which occurs at the beginning, in the position pioneered in the Church of South India and now used in many rites including the Welsh Rite. There is a note to say it can be used after the prayers. Alternative positions are also allowed for the Collect and the Lord's Prayer.

This comparison demonstrates that the mandatory material in Series 3 is not merely 'a bare minimum for a valid rite'. It is a distinctive rite in itself and as such can be used, and is, with no additions for a weekday service. There are occasions when some of this material can be omitted. For example when used in conjunction with Confirmation or the proposed Series 3 form of Infant Baptism it would be permitted to omit the Creed (13) the Prayers (15) and the Penitence (16-19). There may be occasions when a congregation might wish to omit some of this material, of which examples will be examined later, but we should clearly see ourselves as morally, if no longer strictly legally, bound to keep to this structure.

Having then determined the basic structure, we should look at some factors involving our selection from the optional material. It is important to be positive—we decide which material we wish to use rather than what we are going to leave out.

(a) Time

That services should last no longer than an hour is, I believe, a myth that is beginning to be challenged. Many times, options are not used 'because there is not time'. The chief victim of this is the use of the silences, but others include the Commandments, the third reading, the Words of Comfort and the prayers, 'We do not presume' and 'Father of all'. In many circumstances time must be limited because of other services and activities but not in all situations. As many 'charismatic' churches are experiencing, worship can last for several hours with no complaint. Children do not get bored if they are enjoying themselves, and the same is true of adults, and our worship should be enjoyable in the true sense of the word 'joy'.[1]

(b) Theme

A structure, such as is provided by Series 3, enables one to follow a theme through the service. This will determine the use of seasonal material and can of course be taken up in the Sermon, the Prayers and the choice of hymns and other music. It can also determine the use of optional items. The Gloria fits in well with a theme of praise; the Commandments and 'We do

---

1 The 'one hour' service is a modern phenomenon. Paul spoke for a long time at the fellowship in Acts 20. (True, Eutychus fell asleep but that would seem to be a problem of ventilation!) Many accounts of 3rd and 4th century services suggest they took several hours and Cranmer's basic morning pattern (Morning Prayer—Litany—Holy Communion) cannot have lasted less than 2 hours. My plea is not that services ought to be longer but that we should not automatically feel limited by considerations of time in selecting options. In worship people can lose their sense of time.

not presume' with a theme of penitence, whilst the prayer 'Father of all' might well take up an earlier theme. Although the readings are selected on a thematic basis, these need not be the only factors to determine a theme. It might be desired to explore a theme used in weekday housegroups. But above all in this service 'We celebrate and proclaim his perfect sacrifice made once for all upon the cross, his resurrection from the dead and his ascension into heaven; and we look for his coming in glory.'

(c) Music

This is another item to which careful attention must be given when considering the use of the optional material. The rubrics permit almost total freedom in the placing of hymns, but clearly a regular pattern will be essential. Other musical possibilities which should be considered include psalms, including the use of *Psalm Praise*, canticles, choruses, settings for Gloria, Sanctus etc., anthems, solos, organ and instrumental music. This will be determined by the musical tradition of the church and gifts of the individuals available. Hymns are important in expressing the theme and mood of the service. They also serve the useful function of enabling people to stand up and shuffle! There is much to be said for having hymns evenly spaced. For instance a hymn at 14 can be valuable for taking up an aspect of the sermon but also allows people to shift about before the Prayers and the Penitence. Hymns are also helpful but not automatically essential for moving children and taking the collection!

An obvious time for anthems and choir or solo items is during the administration but this is not the only place. Many possibilities exist

> between the readings
> after the sermon, (even if a hymn is to be sung at 14)
> between the confession and absolution
> at the Peace
> at the Breaking of the Bread (some churches sing the Agnus Dei here)
> after the administration

At all these places a time for reflection and meditation can be valuable, and a well-chosen piece of instrumental music or singing can enable this, especially in situations where silence is felt to be inappropriate or seems foreign to the congregation. This might well be a way of introducing silence, at a later stage when people would be better prepared to use it. These are also some of the positions in the service, where in 'charismatic' style worship spontaneous singing will often take place. Here the singing will not seem an intrusion into the structure but rather an enrichment and aid to the worship.

(d) The beginning and the end of the service

Like a sermon, the beginning and the end of a service are most important because they establish the mood and leave a strong impression. Only the minimum of mandatory material is provided. The Collect (6) is the only item required at the beginning and one of the prayers of thanks (39 or 40) and the dismissal (42) at the end. *The Presentation of The Eucharist* makes several suggestions about the use of hymns and purpose of these sections. It must be decided how much emphasis should be made of the entry and exit of the ministers, and what the sections seek to do in the context of the whole service.[1]

It can be seen that once a basic pattern has been established for the use of optional material, most variations from this will be determined by the season of the Church's year or a desire to follow a particular theme throughout a service. Many parishes find that the most satisfactory way of doing this, without causing the congregation to feel uneasy, is to duplicate an order of service to be used in conjunction with the normal booklet. This is of course costly, but many manage to combine this with a list of notices. Words of songs and anthems can also be provided with clear instructions given as to when to turn to the Series 3 booklet.

---

1 An item that needs careful use is the Gloria. G. J. Cuming in *The Eucharist Today* (Ed. R. C. D. Jasper (S.P.C.K., 1974)) p.36, questions 'the uncritical acceptance of tradition' that puts a hymn of praise between two collects. In days when a daily eucharist was the norm, the Gloria marked off Sunday as the special day; for most this significance is now lost. The rubrics suggest that the Kyries should replace the Gloria at penitential seasons, but there might be a good argument for keeping it as a mark of the great festivals. *The Presentation of the Eucharist* suggests that it could be used as an introit at 2 on such occasions.

3. THE WORD AND THE PRAYERS

With the collect of the day the preparation is completed and we are now ready for the first of the two parts of the service—the proclamation of the Word of God through the reading of the Bible and the sermon. Each congregation has to make two main decisions regarding the use of the material provided in this section from 7-13. Firstly whether to have two or three readings and secondly whether to have items between the readings, and if so to decide which material to use. If the Eucharist is to be the main Sunday service that the people attend, then careful consideration must be given to the problem of the the use of the Old Testament.[1]

This must be a theological decision rather than merely a consideration of the practicalities of time.

Concerning the second question of what to do between the readings, there are many possibilities. Care should be taken not to regard these as more musical interludes between proclaiming the Word. The psalms which have traditionally been used here are of course, themselves part of the Word, and whenever possible the psalms provided in the lectionary are related to the theme of the readings.[2]

Many churches find the psalms can be sometimes more effectively said than sung, either altogether or antiphonally (the rubric at 8 seems to favour this). They can of course be sung to the traditional Anglican chant (without Gloria?) or to Gelineau or in a *Psalm Praise* paraphrase. The text also suggests the possibility of hymns or canticles. With the Venite at 2, a psalm at 8, and the Te Deum at 10, it would be possible to make the service almost indistinguishable from Morning Prayer!! In a family setting a chorus or children's song (even with actions) can be used, provided care is taken to relate it to the theme. Whatever material we use it is important both to establish a regular pattern, and not to allow it to detract from the matter in hand—our listening to the Word of God. This can happen if the item is disproportionately long in comparison to the readings, as for example can happen if the whole of the Te Deum or Benedicite or certain hymns are used.

Many possibilities also exist for the presentation of the readings from the Bible. As the preacher may wish to use visual aids to present his message, the same can be done to aid the communication of the written Word. If, however, it would be regarded as gimmickry by the congregation then it is not fulfilling its purpose, and so should not be employed. The purpose

---

[1] If only two lessons are to be used, the Old Testament will be heard at the maximum during only half the year—compulsorily in Advent and the last 5 Sundays in Trinity—and optionally with the epistle from Christmas to the end of Easter.

[2] The *Commentary* on page 16 explains that while they seek to relate the psalms to the theme of the readings, that this is not always possible and sometimes psalms have been chosen to meet the mood and character of the season.

of the Bible is not to entertain, but that does not mean that it cannot be entertaining. Various possibilities are as follows:

1. *Reading by one person.* Cranmer specified that this should be done by the priest, which was being practical, for in many parishes at that time the priest was the only person who could read. It is now accepted practice for lay people to read the epistle and gospel. It does need to be remembered that the gift of reading in public is not possessed by every member of the church. A long rota of lesson readers can be valuable in enabling many people to share in conducting worship, which is highly desirable, but this must not be allowed to be at the expense of communication. The lessons must be read by the people with the special gift of reading in public.

2. *A reading by 2 or 3 people.* This can be a dramatic reading with people reading the words of different characters and with one as narrator. There are many Bible passages that can readily be presented with great effect in this manner.[1]

   More than one voice can also be used in reading many passages from the prophets and the epistles, where rhetorical questions are used, as for instance in Romans or where contrasts are being drawn.

3. *Mime.* The Biblical passage is read in the normal manner, while the story is acted out. This is a favourite with children, but can also be very effective with adults. The parables are obvious material for this treatment as are many dramatic Old Testament stories. Christmas and Easter both provide ideal gospel passages—Luke 2 1-20 and John 20.1-18. No scenery or lighting is needed and only the simplest of costumes and props. This is a useful means of integrating a Sunday School project with the main worship of the church, and the children will never forget the story!

4. *Dramatic presentation.* This is of course far more elaborate, and can therefore be in danger of dominating the service, if it is meant merely to take the place of one reading. If such a presentation is a possibility for the ministry of the Word it could best be done as the whole of sections 7-12.[2]

5. *Use of slides and pictures.* These can be used most effectively to illustrate the passage being read, but only if it can be done without undue disturbance. It is ideal if back projection equipment is already in use but is difficult otherwise.

Another area that can be explored is that of the choice of readings. The lectionary published with Series 3 contains passages of fairly uniform

[1] Darton, Longman and Todd have produced *'The Passion Readings for Three Voices* in the Jerusalem Bible translation, which is intended for the gospel readings in Holy week. This continues an ancient practice in the Roman rite where the long passion gospels were sung by three deacons.

[2] Booklet 35 *Drama in Worship* by Andy Kelso examines this subject in detail.

length. This prevents the reading of a number of stories, which would be considered too long for one reading. The passion readings are the one exception to this, but several Old Testament stories fall into this category. There are also New Testament passages such as some in John's Gospel (the woman at the well, the man born blind, and the raising of Lazarus). There might be occasions when one read the whole of one of these stories and omitted the other readings.[1] One of the means suggested above could be used and if it were still felt to be too long, it could be read in sections with music (very carefully chosen!) in between.

Prayers

The Liturgical Commission invites flexibility in the conduct of the Prayers at 15.

The introductory 'Note' reads 'The Introduction to the specific subjects of prayer is not restricted to the printed forms, "we give thanks for", "we pray for", "we commemorate". Other forms may be used at the discretion of the minister provided they are addressed to God. It is desirable that the subjects of prayer should be expressed briefly.'

Both the *Commentary* and *The Eucharist Today* make suggestions on ways that this material can be used—one continuous prayer without pauses, a litany-style prayer or with extempore prayers introduced at each section by a clergyman or a layman. In both publications great stress is laid on the difference between prayer and biddings. Yet in practice from my own experience this is still not clearly understood. The prayer for the Church and the World is *one* prayer in that it begins 'Almighty God, our heavenly Father' and concludes 'for the sake of your Son, our Saviour Jesus Christ. Amen' and as such it is addressed to God and not the congregation. If biddings are required ('Let us pray for') they should come before the beginning of the prayer.

A number of congregations like to say the set pieces together. If extempore prayer is added it is not necessary at every section. It is quite simple to combine the sections and set pieces so that only 2 or 3 are used at one time.

Who conducts the prayers?

Here again there are many possibilities:

1. A clergyman or Reader.

2. One lay person leading the whole prayer from the congregation.

3. Introduced by a clergyman or Reader but with different lay people leading each section. But some people do find a continual change of voice distracting, particularly if the voices are coming from different directions.

---

[1] In a Maundy Thursday service using this idea, the order of the first part of the service was Hymn (2), Greeting (3), Collects (4, 6), Gospel—Luke 22.14-23.49 (11), silence followed by organ chorale, Sermon (12). This enabled us to hear in one reading the account of the last supper and the crucifixion. The people sat for the reading!

At a Parish or Family Communion, the prayers might be led by members of one family (Father, Mother, 2 children) or an organisation such as Mothers Union, Scouts, Church Council.

Another question that will have to be decided is whether they should be asked to prepare the sections themselves. Lay initiative is obviously to be encouraged, but careful supervision is needed; for instance concerning the difference between prayers and biddings outlined above. It can also be helpful to relate the Prayers to the Ministry of the Word, and to distinguish between items for which we give thanks here, and those 'mighty acts of God' properly included in the Thanksgiving later.

4. Led by one person but with opportunities for general extempore prayer by any member of the church. Here it is essential that acoustic problems are overcome so that all may hear, and the problems of verbosity and awkward silence will have to be faced.

Various aids can also be adopted to make the prayer more related to the congregation. *The Presentation of the Eucharist* suggests taking up themes from the notices, and including them in the prayers. Section 14 could be used for sharing items of church news as well as the mundane notices. Thus a short taped message from a link missionary or former member of the congregation involved in Christian work could be played. News of people prayed for in the previous week could be given.

It is also possible to use visual aids in the prayers. As mentioned, when discussing the readings, one could show slides when a person or particular work is being mentioned, and thus a missionary, a hospital, bishop, a local housing estate, or a national leader. But again it must be stressed that this should only be done if the equipment is already there and in use.

4. THE COMMUNION

The second part of the service begins with 'The Peace' (21, 22). The Commission makes this quite clear:

> 'It is the preliminary of the eucharistic action rather than the conclusion of the act of penitence as in Series 2.'[1]

Liturgically the Peace has been used in several different positions but this is the place adopted in Series 3 and it is desirable to emphasize this transition from the Ministry of the Word to the Communion at this point.[2] The Congregation are required to stand. This might also be the point for the minister to move from the stall to the Holy Table, rather than after the Peace, as is often done. This must be determined by the form to be adopted for the Peace and the geography of the Church.

The rubric suggests that a handclasp or 'similar action' may accompany the Peace, and this has probably caused more difficulty than any other aspect of the service. Many people have been known to reject Series 3 just because they have been required to shake hands and greet those next to them in church. This is because of the traditional 'English reserve' but although it may seem an overemphasised difficulty, it is important to be aware that this seems strange and completely foreign to a large number of people. Great care is needed, and for many churches it needs to be gently encouraged rather than enforced. Below are suggested a number of ways that are used for expressing the Peace among congregations. It may be necessary to accustom a congregation gradually, by using a less free form than might be in the end desired.

1. Words addressed to the Congregation but with no action.

2. A formal handclasp or handshake passed along the rows, beginning with the President and then passed on by wardens and sidesmen. The people can use the same words 'The peace of the Lord be always with you' or perhaps the simpler 'Peace be with you'.

3. Rather than passed along the rows people are asked to greet those on either side of them with a handclasp or handshake. This is of course far speedier than 2.

4. The people are asked to 'greet each other in whatever way you wish'. This prevents the false situation of husbands and wives shaking hands!!

5. Before the Peace there is a 2 minute pause for people to talk to those around them, and this period concludes with the President giving the general Peace.

6. The congregation all join hands while the President gives the Peace.

7. A general informal kiss and hug.

---

[1] *Commentary*, p.20.

[2] This should not be held to preclude having the Peace elsewhere in the service—e.g. at the very beginning or the very end for good reason on occasions.

It might also be useful to list some difficulties that have been encountered in some parishes.

a. Passing the Peace along rows can be lengthy and can tend to peter out towards the back of the church.

b. People can feel embarrassed about remembering a set form of words, even when it is very short.

c. The 'English reserve' is very real.

d. A 'general chat' needs to be directed. It is not a gossip session but should be a real time for sharing.

e. Consideration needs to be given to visitors. Our aim is that they should be made to feel welcome not embarrassed. One does not want to have to make a lengthy explanation of procedure each week.

A valuable point concerning the Peace is made in *The Eucharist Today* where R. J. Halliburton stresses that the Peace must reflect a genuine growing in love and breaking down of divisions in the congregation, which must be going on outside worship. It will otherwise be a purely meaningless ceremony. However, as a congregation does grow together in unity and love, then the Peace will become something very valuable and real to them into which even the stranger will be caught up. Such a movement cannot be imposed—it must grow.

The Taking of the bread and wine

Three sections are included here:

23 *A hymn may be sung and the offerings of the people may be collected and presented*

24 *The bread and wine are brought to the holy table and this sentence may be used.*
> **Yours, Lord . . .** [etc.].

25 *The President takes the bread and the wine.'*

What takes place here will depend very much on our theological understanding of 'Offertory'.[1]

There is no need to associate the collection with the preparing of the bread and wine, if so desired. It can take place at 14. Similarly much can be made of the bringing of the bread and wine to the table with an 'offertory procession', or it can be a purely practical act and so pass virtually unnoticed. If an 'offertory procession' is desired, with its symbolism of the people bringing the bread and wine for the eucharist, then there is much to be said for doing this without a hymn, so that the attention of everybody is focussed upon it. Many parishes like to use different groups to bring up the bread and wine each week, and perhaps relate it to those who have taken part in leading the prayers earlier.

1 See Booklet 10 *A Guide to Series 3* by Peter Dale, p.10.

However, for theological reasons, many parishes will not wish to introduce more symbolism into the service and will want to regard the rubric at 24 in the same way as the rubric for the ordering of the bread and wine before the Prayer of Consecration in 1662. In this case some people like to use the verse from 1 Chronicles in connection with the money rather than the bread and wine as the text strictly suggests.

It is important to distinguish between the rubric at 24 and 25. If these are to be related to the Biblical account of the last supper, 24 technically took place when Peter and John were sent on ahead to prepare the upper room for the supper; 25 was a symbolic act performed by Jesus when the bread was already before him on the table. The liturgical understanding of the Eucharist upon which the Series 3 structure rests is that of repeating the four-fold action of Jesus at the last supper, taking, giving thanks, breaking the bread and sharing. Section 25 is the first part of that. 'It marks the first of the four great actions.'[1]

Series 3 allows a great deal of flexibility in the presentation of the service, but the flexibility does not extend to the structure of the supper, and it is mandatory to accept this four-fold action interpetation. This means the acceptance of the doctrine by which consecration is connected with the whole action rather than the recital of the words of institution. Thus the official *Commentary* and *The Eucharist Today* emphasise that the taking of the bread must take place at 25 and not during the institution narrative as it did in 1662.

If the rubrics of Series 3 had been drafted by Cranmer, there might even have been a negative rubric—similar to that which forbade the elevation of the host in 1549—*'Here the President is not to . . .'*, at the words of institution.

I have laid great stress on this position of the taking because experience suggests that this is not clearly understood by many people, and this would indicate that one of the most fundamental features of Series 3 has not been grasped. Here flexibility of interpretation is not permitted nor should it be encouraged without in practice substantially altering the rite.

It is difficult to emphasise this 'taking' to the congregation since it is done in silence. The Commentary suggests lifting the plate and cup above the table for a moment in silence before beginning the Thanksgiving.

The Thanksgiving and the Breaking of the Bread
There is no optional material, apart from the communion anthems, from sections 26-36. However, flexibility is permitted in the matter of presentation and this needs careful consideration for it reflects the mood of what is happening. *The Presentation of the Eucharist* strongly advocates that there

[1] *The Eucharist Today*" p.91.
[2] See the *Commentary* p.21—'to suggest a 'taking' half way through the Thanksgiving is to frustrate the four-fold sequence which we follow, as well as to invest the reading of the narrative with a purpose and a meaning which we believe to be foreign to its proper use.' See also *The Eucharist Today* p.109.

should be a unity of posture from the Sursum Corda to the Doxology. This is to prevent any suggestion that one part of the prayer is any more sacred than another. Yet still one finds congregations kneeling after the Sanctus, or even after 'It is right to give him thanks and praise'. This destroys the unity of the prayer. *The Presentation of the Eucharist* suggests that people stand for the Thanksgiving, and kneel for the Breaking of the Bread and the Lord's Prayer. This posture will emphasize that the Thanksgiving is a corporate act of the whole church, and not a private prayer.

There are several other possibilities in forms of presenting this section which have been found helpful in emphasizing this corporate aspect of the eucharist.

1. When numbers permit, many have found great advantage in asking the congregation to come and stand around the table before the Peace, and so remain there throughout the Communion, returning to their places when the administration is completed. Of course this will not be possible at a main Sunday service, but could be done on weekdays or for occasions where numbers are small. This practice has good precedent, for in 1662 a rubric before the longer exhortation talks of *'the communicants being conveniently placed for the receiving of the Holy Sacrament.'*

2. The practice favoured by some congregations of everybody saying the section of the Thanksgiving between the acclamations and the Doxology. This again is valuable for those who wish to emphasize that the Thanksgiving is that of the church and not solely the President.

3. The use of a small bread roll rather than individual wafers or pieces of bread. This enables the Breaking of the Bread to be a practical as well as a symbolic act, and vividly demonstrates the words of the 1 Corinthians text that have been attached to it. Sometimes objections are raised to this on practical grounds, but as long as the roll is not too crisp and a large enough plate is used, there should not be any reason why it cannot be done 'decently and in order.'

4. The method of administration. *The Presentation of the Eucharist* stresses that the ministers and the people should receive the Bread and Cup together as one act, but assume the traditional Anglican practice of the people coming up to the area of the table and then receiving the Bread and Cup from the hands of the ministers while either kneeling or standing. Other possibilities have been tried, with the object both of cutting down the time that this takes with a large congregation and of stressing this as being a corporate as well as an individual act.

   a. For some churches the only convenient way of doing the administration is to adopt the method whereby the Bread and Wine is taken to people in their seats who minister to each other along the row. For the Church with 600 communicants and rails that take 12 people, there is no other practical way. Presumably the disciples passed the Bread and Wine around the table at the Last Supper. Great care will be needed to see that this is done with dignity: specially licensed people appointed to take the elements to each row, and an explanation to all present. This method can powerfully demonstrate the concept of each person in the church ministering to his neighbour.

b. Another method is to combine (a) with the traditional method. The people come up to the table and minister to each other. The President gives the elements to the person nearest to him, and the last person ministers to the President.

In both these methods it is important to decide what should be done about non-communicants who have been accustomed to come to the rail for a prayer of blessing.

c. For the ministers with the Bread and the Cup to stand at a suitable place and for the people to file past them receiving the elements. This can often be the most practical method out of doors. It will again need careful organization, as it could look like a cafeteria!! A variation on this is suggested by John Gunstone in *The Charismatic Prayer Group* where the Cup is placed on a small table and each person ministers to himself. This avoids the fear that is very real to some people of dropping the Cup.

Another addition that many congregations value is for the elements to be given with the use of Christian names: 'John, the Body of Christ keep you in eternal life'.[1] With large numbers there is the obvious difficulty that the ministers will not know everybody's name or will forget a name, but there are many congregations in which this is quite possible. In particular if method (a) above is adopted, people should be encouraged to discover the names of those sitting next to them.

Other people however might wish to minister to each other in silence, if they feel the difficulty, mentioned in connection with the Peace, of remembering a set form of words. In this situation the President would say the words generally to the congregation at the beginning.

In any case, whatever the method used, there is much to be said for following out the suggestion of the *Commentary*[2] that the President and other ministers should receive communion themselves last. This means that at 'Draw near' the communicants should immediately come to the appropriate place (not hanging about for the ministers to finish their own private meal first), and at the end the administration to the ministers both covers the departure of the last other communicants and also contains the 'washing up' at the same time. Some people think it more polite also for the presiding persons to receive last themselves. Certainly the rubric was drafted to allow it.

[1] This practice can of course also be done with those receiving a prayer of blessing. 'Mary, may the Lord Jesus bless you.'
[2] See the *Commentary*, p.22.

5. WHAT ABOUT CHILDREN?

The nature of the congregation will make a difference to the use of the material and the way the service is conducted. Thus a Mothers' Union Corporate Communion or a PCC Rededication service might well follow a related theme and involve members in leading various sections such as the readings and the prayers. The latter might also be an occasion in which it would be appropriate to adopt the form of administration suggested at (b) on page opposite.

Concerning the normal Sunday congregation, the main question concerns the presence of children. This poses special problems, which will vary from parish to parish, depending on whether it is considered right that children should be present at the Communion.[1]

However, even though it might be considered desirable that children should be present for the Communion, it is not necessarily right that they should be present throughout the service and another subject tackled in this series has been Christian education and its relation to worship.[2]

In the structure of the Series 3 rite the obvious place for such group instruction is during the ministry of the Word with everybody coming together for the Communion. For many parishes this is an unattainable ideal prevented by lack of suitable accommodation near enough to the main church building. Several parishes, however, are finding that with imaginative use of their present building, what at first seems to be impossible can be done.

It is important to plan carefully when and how groups are to enter and leave. Some will wish the groups to start in their classes and join the congregation later. This has a practical disadvantage in that it will be difficult for them to sit with their parents or possibly even to find them! It is therefore best if the children begin in church with everybody and leave after the opening few minutes. Many parishes like this to happen after the first reading, but is this really the best place? Very often the first lesson will not be relevant to the children or to what they will be doing later. Liturgically the place to leave should be after the Preparation and before the Ministry of the Word. This would be after the Collect (6) and before the first reading. A hymn is not essential for this—it can be done very quickly while the organ is played.

A similar liturgical consideration needs to be applied to their return. If they are to be present for the Communion then rightly they should be there for its beginning, that is before the Peace (see page 16) and a hymn sung at 23 for the collection will be too late. A possible answer is to have a hymn

---

1 Note in Booklet 9 *Patterns of Sunday Worship* Colin Buchanan strongly urges that children should be present, not merely as an inconvenience to be tolerated but in their right as baptised members of the church. This issue is examined in detail by Christopher Byworth in Booklet 8 *Communion, Confirmation and Commitment.* No doubt the debate will continue for the General Synod is now considering the question of the admission of baptized children to communion before confirmation. It is an anomaly to admit children to membership of the church, to allow them to be present at communion, but in the end to deny them the Bread and the Cup.

2 See booklets 11 *Teaching in the Context of Worship* and 31 *Christian Education on Sunday Mornings.* Both these booklets suggest possibilities of combining all-age instruction in small groups with a combined act of worship. 11 is now out of print.

after the prayer of Humble Access (20) and before the Peace. This is the real hinge point of the service. A hymn would not then be needed at 23. The Collection could be taken either during this hymn before the Peace or at 14. If this were to be done the children's collection could be made during their session and presented with the adult collection at 23.

Another possibility is to do the exact opposite—that is for the children to be present for the first half of the service and to leave before the Communion. Thus the first part becomes a family service. This might conclude with a hymn either after the Prayers or before the Peace, with the children going out for special activities while the adults proceed with the Communion. It is, however, open to the objections raised in Booklet 11 since it will involve always teaching the children and adults together. Also if a large number of people is to leave before the Peace the unity of the service could suffer with the Communion becoming a tacked-on 'extra' to the family service rather than the climax of the worship.

The question of children leaving raises the question of the non-communicant adult, who at one time was dismissed before the prayers.[1] This practice has ceased in all but few churches of the Church of England, but the problem is now most acutely felt when the Parish Communion is the only main Sunday service. Present at this may be mourning parties, friends of a 'baptism family', and those whom we could call 'seekers'. For them the ministry of the Word is appropriate, but the fellowship of the Communion, the family meal, may not be. We should be ready to let them stay, or leave, without embarrassment to them or us.

A third possibility is that children will be present throughout the service. This may be the norm for some parishes which do not have a Sunday School, but for many others it will occur only on the great festivals and at holiday times. Here it must be remembered that a family communion is not a children's communion. There are many possibilities for involving children in worship, but care must be taken over audibility. If sufficient use is made of variety in selecting material, even young children can be kept interested, while the creche will be needed for only the very youngest.

Use of the service without communion

This provision is made in the rubrics not only for the situation when there are insufficient communicants or when no priest is available, but as an order of service on its own. One parish uses this format for the monthly non-eucharistic parade service. The same pattern is adopted as would be used at the Parish Communion, using the service either as far as the penitence or the Peace. The sermon comes either at the normal place 12 or after a hymn following the prayers. The collection comes in the hymn following the sermon. This plan has some clear advantages. It integrates the parade service with the weekly worship of the church; economises on books; and provides opportunities to learn musical settings for the Gloria, etc. in a more informal atmosphere.

[1] In early liturgies the dismissal of the catechumens was part of the rite before 'the prayers of the faithful', the second part of the service being the mass of the Faithful. Cranmer had required those who were to communicate to remain in the 'quire'. *'All other (that mynde not to receiue the said Holy Communion) shall departe out of the quire, except the ministers and clerkes.'* (1549 Prayer Book).

6. SERIES 3 PLUS

There are also occasions when it is desired to combine Series 3 with another service or activity. These fall into basically three categories.

1. Something is put into Series 3

This is when it is desired to include another service during the course of a celebration of the Eucharist, often on a Sunday. This has always been the practice with the Ordination service and is the basis of the Coronation service! It is now frequently the practice with the baptism and confirmation services. Provisions are made for this in the official *Commentary* where the principle is established that the additional rite should be placed after the sermon at 12 and the ministry of the Word should remain undisturbed. The Communion is then resumed at the confession or the Peace. New proposed Series 3 services for Infant Baptism, Wedding and the new Funeral service, all include rubrics stating how to incorporate these services into the Communion service. This was also done in Series 2 Confirmation. It is also common practice to include a list of special readings, sentences, collect and proper thanksgiving.

Thus the order of the service with the new proposed form of Infant Baptism might be

    Holy Communion 1-13 (the Creed may be omitted)
    Baptism service (The duties of the parents and Godparents (1) may
        be omitted as are the Lord's Prayer and the Grace (18, 19))
    Intercessions (either Holy Communion 14 or Baptism 17)
    Holy Communion is resumed either with penitence (16) or the
        Peace (21)

This emphasises that it is a Communion service and by inserting all the Baptism service in one place, avoids a lot of switching from book to book. In the Funeral service the commendation (9, 10, 12, 13) is inserted after the administration.[1]

This general principle should be noted when considering placing any extra liturgical ceremony into a service. Examples of this include such things as the commissioning of people in Christian service, and dedication of objects.

2. Series 3 is combined with another service

This is possible with Morning and Evening Prayer,[1] but its main use in the past has been with the wedding service, which has concluded with a Eucharist. There are also certain major parish occasions such as the Institution service or the Consecration or dedication of a building which

---

1 With the proposed wedding service two possibilities are permitted:- one; 'the wedding service within Holy Communion' adopts the above pattern except that the wedding service preface comes at the beginning. The other; 'The Wedding service followed by Holy Communion' follows the pattern in 2 below. It would be interesting to know if weddings have taken place during a Sunday morning Eucharist.

have included the Eucharist. Here careful consideration needs to be given as to whether this is really going to be an appropriate occasion to do this. It must be remembered that this will not be for most people the chief reason why they have gathered. Will it provide a fitting climax to the celebration taking place or will it be merely an addition tacked on the end? If it is decided to combine such a service with Series 3, the Eucharist will begin at the Peace and no extra material should be introduced until the end.[1]

3. Series 3 introduced into another activity

Sometimes there will be a church activity in which it is thought appropriate to celebrate the Eucharist. Such an occasion might be the conclusion of a parish weekend or day study conference. In this situation it is quite possible to bring all the group's activities into the context of the service, and not to isolate the service to the end of the proceedings. A recent *Church Times* report of the Rochester Kirchentag had the headline 'Eucharist lasts $5\frac{1}{2}$ hours'. The Ministry of the Word had involved three discussion groups looking at subjects in depth and the day had concluded with the Thanksgiving. A similar pattern could be used for a parish day conference or even be spread over several days; the preparation at the beginning—the Ministry of the Word with study of the Bible and discussion —a time of prayer and thanksgiving—and the Communion. Such a structure will emphasize the relation of study and worship. At the last supper many activities took place within the structure of the Jewish liturgy (probably the passover) that was taking place.

There are also situations in which one might wish to use Series 3 in the context of a meal. In a parish this will be a rare event, though in some places it is becoming a tradition for Maundy Thursday, and also might be appropriate on a houseparty. An example of such a meal is quoted in Booklet 19 *Agapes and Informal Eucharists* by Trevor Lloyd. The pattern he suggests there could easily be adapted to the Series 3 text. The first and main course coming before the ministry of the Word, and the sweet course after the Prayers.

Series 3 could also be used in a house group. Some of the issues that this involves are discussed by John Gunstone in *The Charismatic Prayer Group.* Clearly close discipline is needed if the service is to be used in home settings, but there are occasions on which this might be considered appropriate.[2]

In a house group, corporate Bible study can come at 12 in the place of the sermon, and a time of open prayer at 15.

Having given examples of ways in which Series 3 can be used in situations other than the regular Sunday or weekday worship of the church, it must be reiterated that great care is needed over this. Permitted flexibility should not lead to the license of using the service on inappropriate occasions. The narrative of its institution by the Lord is sufficient reminder of the importance and solemnity of this joyous occasion which requires careful spiritual and practical(!) preparation.

[1] See *Commentary* p.28 and Series 3 Morning and Evening Prayer p.4.
[2] For an example of combining Series 3 with the Institution service see Booklet 15 *Institutions and Inductions* by Trevor Lloyd.